COZYCOLOR
WHAT'S INSIDE

BOTANICAL GARDEN

COZYCOLOR

WHAT'S INSIDE

BOTANICAL GARDEN

COLOR TEST PAGE

COLOR TEST PAGE

BOTANICAL GARDEN

COZYCOLOR

REVERSE COLORING BOOK

Published By
Rainbow Stone
Publishing

Pixels Pete

BOTANICAL GARDEN

COZYCOLOR

REVERSE COLORING BOOK

____

THIS BOOK BELONGS TO

PEACE ROSE PRIME

EDEN ROSE

DOUBLE DELIGHT ROSE

TEA ROSES

ANGEL FACE ROSE

CALLA LILIES

TIGER LILIES

ORIENTAL LILIES

LILY PADS

MAJESTIC MILTS

SUNNY DAZE

GOLDEN GLOW

SUNSHINE BOUQUET

SUNSHINE BLOOMS

DAISY DELIGHT

MEADOW BLOOM

BLOOMIN' DAISIES

DREAMY DAISIES

SPRING FLING

TULIP TRIO

TULIP BLOOMS

TIPTOEING TULIPS

TULIP TANGO

Made in the USA
Coppell, TX
16 April 2023

15651276R00044